Redemption Through the Scriptures:

Study Guide

Books by Paul J. Bucknell

Allowing the Bible to speak to our lives today!

Overcoming Anxiety: Finding Peace, Discovering God

Reaching Beyond Mediocrity: Being an Overcomer

The Life Core: Discovering the Heart of Great Training

The Godly Man: When God Touches a Man's Life

Redemption Through the Scriptures // Study Guide

Godly Beginnings for the Family

Principles and Practices of Biblical Parenting

Building a Great Marriage

Christian Premarital Counseling Manual for Counselors

Relational Discipleship: Cross Training

Running the Race: Overcoming Lusts

Genesis: The Book of Foundations

Book of Romans: The Living Commentary

Book of Romans: Bible Studies

Book of Ephesians: Bible Studies

Walking with Jesus: Abiding in Christ

Inductive Bible Studies in Titus

1 Peter Bible Study Questions: Living in a Fallen World.

Take Your Next Step into Ministry

Training Leaders for Ministry

Study Guide for Jonah: Understanding God's Heart

Check out these valuable resources at www.foundationsforfreedom.net

Redemption Through the Scriptures: Study Guide

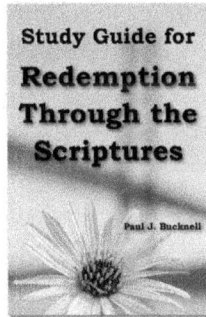

Paul J. Bucknell

"Their Redeemer is strong,
the LORD of hosts is His name."
(Jeremiah 50:34)

Redemption Through the Scriptures: Study Guide

Printed:
ISBN-10: 1619930560
ISBN-13: 978-1-61993-056-8

Digital eBooks:
ISBN-10: 1-61993-010-2
ISBN-13: 978-1-61993-010-0

Redemption Through the Scriptures
Printed: ISBN-13: 978-1-61993-028-5
Digital: ISBN:-13: 978-1-61993-011-7

www.foundationsforfreedom.net
Pittsburgh, Pennsylvania,15212 USA

The NAS Bible is used unless otherwise noted. Scripture quotations taken from the New American Standard Bible®, Copyright © 1960, 1962, 1963, 1968, 1971, 1972, 1973, 1975, 1977, 1995 by The Lockman Foundation. Used by permission. (www.Lockman.org)

Contact Paul at info@foundationsforfreedom.net. For other resources: handouts, videos, audios and powerpoint slides see Discipleship #3 Digital Library (D3).

Table of Contents

Introduction...9

#1 Study: The Plan of Redemption...........................13

Study Questions
Advanced Questions

#2 Study: The Purpose for Redemption 19

Study Questions
Advanced Questions

#3 Study: The Proclamation of Redemption............25

Study Questions
Advanced Questions

#4 Study: The Scope of Redemption.........................31

Study Questions
Advanced Questions

#5 Study: The Scheme of Redemption.....................37

Study Questions
Advanced Questions

#6 Study: The Design of Redemption.......................43

Study Questions
Advanced Questions

#7 Study: The Damage Requiring Redemption........49

    Study Questions

    Advanced Questions

#8 Study: The Redeemer Brings Redemption 55

    Study Questions

    Advanced Questions

#9 Study: The Price of Redemption...........................61

    Study Questions

    Advanced Questions

#10 Study: The Preciousness of Redemption 67

    Study Questions

    Advanced Questions

#11 Study: Delight in Joint Service...........................73

    Study Questions

    Advanced Questions

#12 Study: Determined to Share His Holiness.........79

    Study Questions

    Advanced Questions

#13 Study: Desire for a Loving Relationship 83

    Study Questions

    Advanced Questions

#14 Study: Deeper Fellowship with our Lord...........89

    Study Questions
    Advanced Questions

#15 Study: Summary of Redemptive Truths.............95

    Study Questions
    Advanced Questions

#16 Study: Summary of Redemptive Restoration...101

    Study Questions
    Advanced Questions

Introduction

This study guide serves as a companion volume for the book, *Redemption Through the Scriptures*. It can be used for adult classes as well as small group studies or personal development. *Redemption Through the Scriptures* specializes in offering a biblical and chronological perspective of God's redemptive saving program, highlighting more than ten salvation themes.

Each of the sixteen studies use 3 to 5 major scripture passages to develop the chapter's main theme. Two sets of questions: Study Questions and Advanced Questions provide the flexibility needed to make most of these studies whether for personal profit, class instruction, or small group studies.

Study Questions provides a general review of the chapter material and aids in learning and applying the basic truths found from the relevant scripture passages. The answers are found rather easily when carefully reading through the chapter. We place a lot of emphasis on application due to Jesus' own words: "Everyone who hears these words of Mine and does not at on them, will be like a foolish man who built his house on the sand" (Matthew 6:26).

Advanced Questions differs from the basic set in several ways. First, these questions take the salient chapter points and expand them so that they shed light on other areas of studies, better integrating these truths into our personal lives and beliefs. Second, they require more thought. The answers are present but, one must train oneself to logically think through and apply these truths. Third, they take more time! Prepare to have a place for your own notes. This set of questions turns an enjoyable reading of this book into a class! Lastly, the section sometimes requires projects to be done. These projects, sometimes requiring further research, reveal the way that we have come to important conclusions made in this book.

Small group usage: This book can be used to lead a small group discussion since each chapter is centered around a redemptive theme developed from the scriptures. The attendees might or might not read the chapters. If so, they can read the chapter before or after the discussion times, each with their own advantage. If not, the leader can carefully prepare the most appropriate questions for the group after briefly introducing the point of the chapter–provided at the beginning of the study. Go through the study questions and pick the most relevant ones and focus on one or two good application points, always highlighting the main theme of each chapter in light of the whole purpose of the book. Read through the advanced questions for other possible approaches.

Teaching resources: There are many other resources designed for this course including: handouts, beautiful powerpoint slides, and audio/visual materials for selected chapters. All and more can be found in the Discipleship #3 Digital Library (D3). Make most of the many diagrams and colorful graphics that further clarify the power truths of the scripture.

Please do join me in delighting in this amazing story of God's love and grace!

Paul J. Bucknell
Pittsburgh, PA, USA

#1 Study: The Plan of Redemption

Redemption Through the Scriptures

Did you ever wonder why Jesus needed to die to bring salvation? By taking a deeper look into the meaning and usage of the word 'redemption,' the relevancy of the salvation plan becomes a powerful force in our lives. Though the word 'redemption' no longer communicates to us its hidden connotation of slavery, it serves as a powerful liberating truth behind the cross, making manifest God's righteousness, compassion, wisdom, and faithfulness through the purchase of His people with the blood of Christ Jesus.

Study Questions

1) Share about something special that you wanted, that you bought, and the price you paid for it.

2) What is one chief reason for the weakness found in the church today around the world?

3) Write from memory the two diagrams: "My Plans" and "God's Plans." Use them to explain the weakness in the church. (Review them first if you need to!)

4) Do you live more by the "Me" plan or "God" plan? Explain.

5) What does the word 'redemption' mean?

6) What two senses does the word redeem have?

7) Why does the Christian church use the words: redeem and redemption so frequently?

8) List a few means by which man tries to restore harmony with God (or a Great Spirit being). Why are these methods ineffective?

9) Explain how the scene of man's original disobedience hints at man's chief spiritual problem. Why did the disobedience in the Garden of Eden bring such great consequences?

10) Explain Jesus' two step explanation of man's problem from John 8.

11) How does Colossians 1:13-14 show us both the problem of the human race and how redemption solves that problem?

12) Summarize why Jesus needed to die on the cross. Connect your explanation with the word 'redemption.'

13) On a scale from 1 to 5 (5 being the strongest), choose the number that best reflects how redemption, as explained above, influences your life.

Advanced Questions

1) What are we redeemed from and for? Briefly introduce a diagram showing the eternal plan of redemption.

2) Do a Bible search for the word "redeem*" (around 102 usages) and group them according to their uses including: real life situations, theological concepts and other categories as needed. Write down at least three observations.

✦

✦

✦

3) Why are the words: 'redeem' and 'redemptive' so commonly used in the church, though not so much in our culture? What is perhaps a better way to explain this 'foreign' word 'redemption' and its associated ideas?

4) In light of what we know about redemption, is it good to accept the plurality of religions? Aren't there many ways to God? Why or why not?

5) Identify three ways popular phrases used to assert man's freedom from moral constraint. Only a complete understanding protects us from the evil one's treacherous bait.

✦

✦

✦

#2 Study: The Purpose for Redemption

Redemption Through the Scriptures

God was not content to create an army of slaves bound to do whatever they're commanded to do. Instead, He desired the intimacy of friends so that we, both in eternity and on earth, can enjoy the good work that He's designed for us to do. There is no better place to see this than in the Old and New Covenants that God put in place to restore the partnership between Him and His people.

Study Questions

1) What positive pictures do we have of the relationship between God and man in the first three chapters of Genesis?

2) What is so surprising of God's willingness to work with people?

3) Once the question of God's willingness to help people is accepted, what is the next question that pops up?

4) What is so special about the Old Covenant (Mosaic)? Use the chart on Numbers 2 to explain.

5) Where was the Old Covenant given? How does it begin and how does this give us an idea about the relationship God wants with those under the covenant?

6) Where did the term 'new covenant' originate from?

7) Provide three ways the New Covenant is superior to the Old Covenant. Which one means the most to you? Why?

✦

✦

✦

8) What is so significant about the two pictures of God's purpose for redemption?

✦

✦

9) Concisely state the purpose of redemption.

10) Use three adjectives to describe the kind of relationship you believe God wants with you? As time allows, please explain.

Advanced Questions

1) If someone suggests that the God of the Old Testament is mean and unpleasant, how might you answer that person?

2) On a scale of 1 to 10, would you say your relationship with God is close, 1 being not so and 10 being very close. Briefly explain your choice.What kind of fruit might appear from being close to God? Give at least three possible fruits.

-
-
-

3) Why do you think God gives us commands? Is it merely because He wants His ways or is there some greater purpose? Read 1 John 5:3 and compare how this verse compares to your attitude.

4) The modern church is weak due to her focus on her gained freedom. What has she been set free from and what has she been freed for?

   +

   +

5) Study John 15:1-16 and describe at least three pictures of intimacy that God purposes to have with His people through Jesus Christ.

   +

   +

✦

6) Why do many people despise marriage as God designed?
Why does God use marriage as a picture of His
relationship with His people? Identify at least four
points.

✦

✦

✦

✦

#3 Study: The Proclamation of Redemption

God relates to individuals in different ways. This is seen specifically in how He speaks to them. However much God might speak to us, though, we need to understand and embrace His thoughts (i.e. His truth) to make them ours. Each word becomes significant in the way He reveals and completes His plans.

Study Questions

1) Try to describe what happens when you speak. Explain how it happens and what occurs in the end when someone hears you speaking to them.

2) How did God create the world? Find at least three verses from Genesis chapter 1 that refers to God's Word.

3) In the first few chapters of Genesis we see God speaking to Adam and Eve. What did He say? How did He communicate with them?

4) Genesis 4 is especially interesting to study due to Cain's stubbornness. How does God address Cain here? What general conclusions about God can we make through this conversation?

5) What can we learn from Genesis 12:1-3 and God's desire, not only for Abram, but for His relationship with people around the world? How did God communicate this? What was the fulfillment dependent upon?

6) Did you ever dialogue back and forth with God? About what? What was the result?

7) There are two kinds of revelation from God: His works and His words. Read through Psalm 19 and see which part is associated with which kind of revelation. Write down at least one observation from each section. Describe we can be learned about God from it.

✦ Psalm 19:   His words –

+ Psalm 19:   His works –

8) Read Jeremiah 33:10-11. This is just one of many prophetic passages often depicted by words like "Thus says the Lord." What did the Lord say in these verses? How did the Lord communicate these things?

9) Relate one time when reading the Psalms or Proverbs that you could really identify with what was being said. How is it that God used His Word to strengthen and help you.

10) Memorize Hebrews 1:1-3. Identify at least three things these verses state about Jesus. Note especially how God speaks through Jesus.

   +

   +

   +

11) What are some pictures of the church given in the scriptures that show the intimacy and need for close communication?

12) God's people are instructed to pray without stopping (1 Th 5:17). How is prayer related to our relationship and communication with God?

13) God's people are called a royal priesthood (1 Peter 2:9)? What does it mean and imply?

14) The Bible plays a very important part of our Christian lives? Why? Identify Paul's key points in 2 Timothy 3:16-17.

15) Do you have a habit of listening to God? Do you anticipate that God wants to speak to you each day, whether in encouraging or discouraging times? Explain.

16) Do you pray and carry out your role of royal priesthood? What does it practically mean to you?

17) Intimacy and closeness are seen through the conversations one has with others. What is the standard for New Testament believers in their relationship with God? Why? Including the personal times with God in praise, prayer, listening to God's word during the last

week, would you say that you are where God wants you to be? Explain.

Advanced Questions

1) What can we learn about parenting through the Lord's dealing with Adam, Eve and Cain in Genesis 2-4?

2) Look up the number of times the phrase, "Thus says the Lord" in either KJB or NASB concordance (e.g. Biblegateway.com) is used. What are your first observations?

3) Contrast the books of Joshua and Judges. What makes them so different? Look at Judges 2:1-10 and show the contrast between Joshua's generation and post-Joshua generation. What made the big difference?

4) Memorize John 1:1. What does it mean that Jesus is called the Word of God?

5) How much time do you talk with your spouse? Many husbands hardly speak to their wives! From the example

of the intimacy Christ (the bridegroom) desires to have with the church (the bride), what kind of communication should go on between spouses?

6) How are believers to pass on God's words (Word of God)? What do we (or should we) expect to happen as we do this?

7) Christian growth can be measured by how readily we receive God's Word, are personally changed and pass His truth on to others. How would you evaluate these three aspects in your life? Which area is your church good at? Which area is it weak in?

* Receive God's Word

* Changed by God's Word

* Pass God's Word on

#4 Study: The Scope of Redemption

Redemption Through the Scriptures

God loves His growing family. Even though Adam's failure seemed to have cut off this hope, God's tremendous and patient work throughout history will bring a great multitude into His kingdom, creating a family with whom to share His great riches.

Study Questions

1) Why is Genesis 3:15 sometimes called the proto-Gospel?

2) Name two places in Genesis where the Lord commands people to "be fruitful and multiply." What is different about their situations?

   ✦

   ✦

3) How would you describe the words, "be fruitful" and "multiply" in your own words?

4) What is the difference between God's creation plan and His redemptive plan?

5) Why did God not start completely new after the flood (like eliminate sinful Noah and create sinless man)?

6) The Lord caused the people to have different languages at the Tower of Babel (Gen 11:1-9). Name at least two possible reasons He did this.

   ✦

   ✦

7) When God seeks to bless Abram in Genesis 17:4-7, what promises does He give him?

8) How is Genesis 22:17-18 linked to what we now know as missions (in the church)?

9) Name two significant observations from Galatians 3:16.

   ✦

   ✦

10) How is the phrase "in Christ" linked to the promise of the seed?

11) Once Christ died on the cross, the Spirit of God mobilized the church. Identify what was significant about each of these passages in the thrust to reach out to the nations.

   • Acts 2

   • Acts 8

   • Acts 10

   • Acts 13

12) What does unreached people mean? Where did it get its meaning?

13) What is everyone looking for in Revelation 5:1-9? Did they find it? Why was it so important?

14) What connects the phrase from "From every tribe and tongue and people and nation" (5:9) with the promises made to Abraham in Genesis 17 and 22?

15) What would your life be like if God started a completely new creation at the time of Noah's flood? Think about your own life, problems and all. Thank God for His patience! Think about one person you could be more patient toward, then be patient!

Advanced Questions

1) Why didn't God just start anew when He destroyed the world by the flood? Wasn't the same problem going to happen?

2) From what Scripture passage(s) does the notion of missions in the church derive from? Why does Piper say it is a "temporary necessity"?

3) Study Romans 11:13-26 and identify a few key points about how God is working with both the Jews and Gentiles (non-Jews).

4) How is this redemptive plan connected to Jesus' command to make disciples of all nations (Matthew 28:18-20)?

5) What place does God's mission to reach to the ends of the world have on your church and life?

#5 Study: The Scheme of Redemption

Redemption Through the Scriptures

God's kingship and authority over mankind was given to Adam but then subverted to Satan. God regained control by becoming a man and living righteously. Christ rules, both now and in the future.

Study Questions

1) Name at least one key redemptive fact from Ephesians 1:9-10.

2) Why is it that Jesus did not choose the easy path (see Matthew 4:8-10)?

3) State in your own words how Satan gained authority over men's hearts and the earth.

- Men's hearts:

- The earth:

4) Use at least ten adjectives to describe Satan's "domain of darkness" (Colossians 1:13-14). (Note: They are not found in these verses.)

5) What does "slaves to sin" from Romans 6:20 mean?

6) List four things man lost?

-

-

-

-

7) Why is the city generally more resistant to God's ways?

8) Draw the diagram of the Israelite kings including the dates. Be sure to explain the difference between the unified and divided kingdoms.

9) Why was it so wrong for the Israelites to ask for a king (1 Samuel 8:6-8)? After all, Samuel's sons became corrupted.

10) List one of the righteous Old Testament kings. What made him good?

11) List one of the unrighteous Old Testament kings. What made him evil?

12) Is the term 'second Adam' used in the Bible? Why is it referred to?

13) Why is it so important that Jesus is described both as the Lamb and the Lion?

14) Do you think of Jesus as king much? What is one way you can better describe your thanks to Him for so greatly caring for you and making you His own? (Thank Him!)

Advanced Questions

1) Is Jesus king over all now ? On what basis do you state that?

2) Why do some believers state He doesn't rule now by saying, "He doesn't physically rule over the earth?"

3) In what ways does the evil one affect man's life in today's world?

4) Do the rule of governments pay attention to God's judgments and ways? Explain, giving examples for at least two governments you are familiar with (on whatever level, past or present).

5) What is the biggest lesson you learn from the Old Testament kings? Why so?

6) Restate what man needs to be redeemed from (e.g. four things man lost) and support each with at least one Bible verse.

 ✦

 ✦

 ✦

 ✦

7) Explain what each term, Adam and last Adam, means and their implication (Romans 5:12-21).

 ✦

 ✦

#6 Study: The Design of Redemption

Redemption Through the Scriptures

Redemption was planned before time began. Prophecies are God's way of planting promises and hope into His people's minds, reminding them of His plans. There are literally underlined hundreds of these prophecies, especially if we count how several prophecies can stem from one verse. God intensifies our curiosity and shows us that even man's best is inadequate to reach God's goals of redemption. God wants us to live in full appreciation of His gift of Christ (John 3:16).

Study Questions

1) How does Ephesians 1:3-4 show us, without any doubt, that Jesus Christ coming into the world was not God's second best choice but His best plan?

2) There are many religions. Why is it, then, that this study of prophecies convinces us that Jesus Christ is the only Savior?

3) How are prophecies like hints? What is characteristic about the biblical prophecies describing Christ and His work?

4) Memorize 1 Peter 1:10-12. State at least one special observation from these verses.

5) State at least one fact about Christ's birth from the following prophecies.

   ✦ Micah 5:2

   ✦ Isaiah 7:14

   ✦ 2 Samuel 7:12-13

6) Make at least one aspect of Christ's death from the following prophecies.

✦   Psalm 22:1, 14-18

✦   Isaiah 53:4-6,10

✦   Zechariah 11:12-13

7) Look at these prophecies of Christ's resurrection. Name at least one fact from each prophecy.

✦   Psalm 22:22

✦   Psalm 16:10

✦   Jonah 1:17

8) Make at least one observation about Christ's rule from the following prophecies.

✦   Zechariah 9:9

✦   Isaiah 9:6-7

✦   Psalm 2:6-7

9) Do you use the phrase, "Jesus is Lord"? Do you personally think of Jesus ruling now in His kingdom with all the authority in heaven and earth? Share how these truths do or do not influence your life thought and decisions.

Advanced Questions

1) Why would God allow an imperfect creation to arise? If God didn't like sin and rebellion, why did He create a world where they could evolve?

2) Identify the key phrases about redemption found in Ephesians 1:3-8.

3) The above prophecies are just a small portion of all the prophecies quoted in the New Testament from the Old Testament. Scan through the New Testament and find five other prophecies not used above. Discover the reason they were quoted. Afterwards, find and read their original Old Testament source. Note any special observations.

✦

✦

✦

✦

✦

#7 Study: The Damage Requiring Redemption

Without sin there is no need for redemption. Without the fall, there is no redemptive lift. Although Satan temporarily seems to frustrate God's plan to have a group of people devoted to Him and be glad in His presence, God unveils an encompassing plan that defeats Satan's worst plans and reveals that the redemption of his people was planned all along.

Study Questions

1) Fill in the blank, "In order to _____ the problem, one must first understand the problem."

2) Why is the Genesis 3 account so critical to understanding redemption?

3) Was it good for man to have an ability to choose? Explain.

4) Fill in the blanks. Man went from innocent to

_____ to _____ to deceived to sinful.

5) List the three images Isaiah uses in Isaiah 5:24 to describe the barrenness resulting from the fall.

   ✦

   ✦

   ✦

6) What two reasons does Isaiah give that cause this barrenness?

   ✦

   ✦

7) List at least four descriptions of the sinner from Romans 3:10-12.

   ✦

   ✦

   ✦

   ✦

8) Why is the phrase, "There is no one who seeks God" so significant?

9) What are the three stages of the redemptive plot (also see the diagram on page 136)?

   ✦

   ✦

   ✦

10) What are three descriptions of fallen man from Ephesians 2:1-3?

✦

✦

✦

11) How does the state of being spiritually 'dead' make religion and 'good works' ineffective in saving man?

12) What phrase from Ephesians 2:4-6 means most to you?

13) Think about your devotion to the Lord. What has the Lord done for you without you deserving it? How should this shape your relationship with the Lord? Name one thing you will do to express this grace (e.g. Write or sing a song, a poem, tell someone about His love, etc.).

14) What is God's supreme purpose for the redemptive plan (Ephesians 2:7)?

15) What is the significance of the phrase, "Bought with the price" from 1 Corinthians 6:20?

16) Think back on your sinfulness. What were you like? What has God saved you from? If you were young when saved, try to imagine how the problems would get worse as you aged, if you had not by God's grace changed. Thank the Lord for His grace.

Advanced Questions

1) What key parts of the redemptive plan would be missing if we did not have Genesis 3's description of the fall?

2) List a few explanations, biblical or otherwise, for the wickedness of mankind (i.e. Why is there war?)?

   ✦

   ✦

   ✦

3) Ask at least three people why people do wicked things? Write down their comments.

   ✦

✦

✦

4) How do we know from Ephesians 2:8-10 that God has more in mind in His redemption plan than just forgiving us from our sins?

5) How does the rule of Satan differ from the rule of the Lord God? Include in your answer the variant purposes, means, relationships, characteristics, etc.

   ✦ Rule of Satan

   ✦ Rule of God

6) Compare how religions try to generally address the sin problem but only the OT/NT scriptures proclaim this salvation through Jesus Christ and His work on the cross. Use at least two religions as reference.

   ✦

   ✦

#8 Study: The Redeemer Brings Redemption

Redemption Through the Scriptures

People need God's help. Man's sin revealed mankind's desperate plight. Fortunately, God has and does intervene. He waits for man's cry and intercedes for His people, diminishing the impact of sin and judgment by pointing us to the Redeemer Jesus Christ.

Study Questions

1) All the images of heroes, helpers, redeemers and saviors that we have in the world point to the wonderful Redeemer, _____ _____.

2) What is it that Satan tries to do to the unbeliever?

3) Explain how the Lord helped Peter trapped in jail waiting to be killed (see Acts 12:1-7).

4) What were the two things King Hezekiah did upon hearing it was the end of his life (Isaiah 38)?

✦

✦

5) Why is it important to recognize one's unresolvable guilt before the Lord?

6) Who powerfully refuted the Jews in public, demonstrating by the Scriptures that "_____ was the Christ" (Acts 18:28).

7) What is significant about the Book of Ruth? How is it connected to the hope for a coming Redeemer?

8) What was so significant about Job's words, "And as for me, I know that my Redeemer lives, and at the last He will take His stand on the earth" (Job 19:25)?

9) Memorize one verse from Psalms or Proverbs that speaks about the Redeemer. Write it down and explain what makes that verse so meaningful?

10) Why is the term 'Redeemer' is increasingly associated with God the Savior?

11) Explain how God's securing coverings for Abram and Eve is so noteworthy.

12) List four of the seven articles of special clothing for Aaron the High Priest. Why did the high priest have to wear such special clothing?

✦

✦

✦

✦

13) Provide at least one verse that indicated Jesus occupied the High priest's role.

14) Why do we call Jesus the Redeemer even though the term Redeemer is not used in the New Testament?

15) What are the two main truths from 1 Timothy 2:5 that is relevant to this discussion?

◆

◆

16) Can you give a situation when you cried out to God for help and found His help as Redeemer? Explain.

Advanced Questions

1) Explain the importance of Shiloh from Jacob's prophesy.

2) Study Melchizedek and what the scriptures say about him (Gen 14, Ps 110:4; Heb 5:6-10; Heb 7:1-17).

3) Is there any impossible situation for you or others for which you can now call upon the Lord?

4) Why is public nudity wrong?

5) Explain the biblical chronological line of intimacy with God and relate how it is related to what one wears. (Hint: He starts by living in God's presence covered with God's light and glory.)

#9 Study: The Price of Redemption

Redemption Through the Scriptures

There are specific reasons that faith in Jesus' death on the cross only can take away our sins–not other religions, sacrifices, saviors or good works. "Jesus said to him, 'I am the way, and the truth, and the life; no one comes to the Father, but through Me'" (John 14:6). Death is due each of us because of our inherited sin and our own disobedience. We earned this judgment with our disobedience through Adam. Christ's sacrifice is the only sacrifice that satisfies God's wrath and allows us to keep living.

Study Questions

1) List at least three words to describe death and its consequences.

✦

✦

✦

2) Is death natural? Explain.

3) How did sin enter the world? Use Bible verses to explain.

4) Explain how physical death is different from spiritual death.

5) Does judgment end with physical death? Why or why not?

6) If God said man would die if he ate the forbidden fruit, why then, is there a human race?

7) Why did God's redemptive plan need to deal with man's sin?

8) Why did Jesus die on the cross?

9) Where do we first see God's concern for helping man and not merely carry out His immediate judgment?

10) Explain the words, "He Himself bore our sins in His body on the cross" from 1 Peter 2:24. Why did Jesus have to bear our sins?

11) What is the difference between guilt and guilty feelings? Which one is God primarily concerned with and why?

  ✦ Guilt

  ✦ Guilty feelings

12) From Hebrews 9:17-22 tell why Jesus needed to die on the cross.

13) Similarly, from Galatians 3:13-14 tell why Jesus needed to die on the cross.

14) What does propitiation mean? Why is it relevant to this discussion?

15) What makes Genesis 15:1-6 such a key passage to help us understand how a person is saved?

16) Use Romans 4:1-5 to explain why a person must not trust in his own works to gain acceptance before God.

17) How is it possible that Jesus' death can bring forgiveness to the human race?

18) Summarize how Jesus' death is related to our sin, faith and redemption plan.

19) Select what you believe and place your confidence in:

   ✦ _____ Jesus' death a sacrificial substitutional atonement

   ✦ _____ God generally demonstrated His tolerance for sinners.

   ✦ _____ (Other; explain)

Advanced Questions

1) How might we use this discussion of death to speak to evolutionists who insist on death being a natural phenomena?

2) How do guilty feelings help us? How can they ruin us?

3) How would you counsel someone facing persistent guilty feelings?

4) What additional insights on the atonement do you gain from each use of the word propitiation (Romans 3:25; Hebrews 2:17; 1 John 2:2; 4:10)?

5) What is so different in the way Jesus acts as the Savior in the two verses below? What is theologically significant about them?

   ✦ "Therefore, He had to be made like His brethren in all things, that He might become a merciful and faithful high priest in things pertaining to God, to make propitiation for the sins of the people" (Heb 2:17).

✦ "He Himself is the propitiation for our sins; and not for ours only, but also for those of the whole world" (1 John 2:2).

6) What are various theological views of the atonement? How are they different and why are they significant? (A good in-depth book: *The Atonement* by A.A. Hodge.)

#10 Study: The Preciousness of Redemption

Redemption Through the Scriptures

The sacrifice was important but so were the altars where the sacrifice was offered. There is an interesting series of connections pointing to the place where Jesus would be offered up, and it's all part of God's design. Two very different Old Testament sacrifices and their surrounding events prefigured the greatest altar of all where the final offering of Christ took place as predicted.

Study Questions

1) What is something precious that you lost? What made it precious to you?

2) How do we know Jesus' death on the cross was no mere accident (Acts 2:22-23)?

3) Why did Abraham offer up his only son, Isaac (Genesis 22:1-6)?

4) What do you think was hard about Abraham offering up Isaac?

5) Two main illustrations from the offering up of Isaac help us better understand the significance of Christ's death on the cross. Explain each.

✦ Only son

✦ Substitute sacrifice

6) What did the wood that Isaac carried up the mountain represent?

7) What is the Hebrew term for 'God provides'? What is the significance of it?

8) What are at least three ways the event with Abraham and David were different?

✦

✦

✦

9) Why did so many people die because of David's counting sin?

10) Why is this incident with David so significant with respect to the overall redemptive plan?

11) Why did the angel of the Lord stop outside Jerusalem?

12) List the 3 significant events that took place on Mt. Moriah.

✦

✦

✦

13) In the three events above, how is it that God intervenes? What is similar?

14) David's sacrifice averted God's judgment upon _____ is like Christ's sacrifice that averts judgment upon the _____. (Please complete.)

15) List at least two scriptures that refer to Jesus as the Son.

   ✦

   ✦

16) How does the Chinese character for righteousness summarize the Gospel?

17) Memorize Galatians 4:6. Write it down.

18) How does John 3:14-16 help us understand how to gain the forgiveness of sins through Jesus?

19) Do you personally believe all your sins are fully forgiven? Even your worst ones? If so, when did you come to think this? On what basis do you believe it?

Advanced Questions

1) Read a few articles on the whereabouts of 'Golgotha and Moriah.' Write down your conclusions.

2) Do a word study on the word 'begotten.' What is significant about these ten NT verses about God's Son?

3) How does a 'born' son and 'begotten' son differ?

4) Do you think the place Jesus hung is the same as Abraham's offering of Isaac and David's sacrifice. Explain why or why not.

5) Explain the meaning of the substitutional atonement using Abraham's illustration.

6) Why are Muslims so resistant for God to have a Son?

7) State the doctrine of the trinity and provide at least three verses explaining or otherwise testifying to it.

#11 Study: Delight in Joint Service

God's purpose for this world is not just to reign but to create a great host of people to co-rule with Him. By living a life inflamed by God's holy presence, they intercede on the behalf of the weak and needy, ministering God's Word. Redemption cannot be understood unless we see its greater purpose fulfilled in the fellowship and joint service of God's people.

Study Questions

1) What is the purpose of God to purchase a people of God for Himself? (You might stimulate your thinking by reflecting what goes through your mind when you buy expensive items.)

2) How is the *Parable of The Great Pearl* identified with redemption?

3) What in Acts 20:28 reveals God's delight to work in and through His people the church?

4) From Genesis 1-2 state what God expected man and woman to do?

5) List five people in the Bible with whom God spoke and the work that He requested them to do. (Include at least two individuals that are not mentioned above.)

   ✦

   ✦

   ✦

   ✦

   ✦

6) Describe at least three characteristics of how the Lord worked with Joshua.

   ✦

✦

✦

7) What are at least two principles that we discover from 2 Chronicles 7:12-14 about how God desires to work in and through human beings?

✦

✦

8) Reflect on the "The Work of Proclamation" chart (right). What had to happen before sinful man could carry out the works of the Living God? Why?

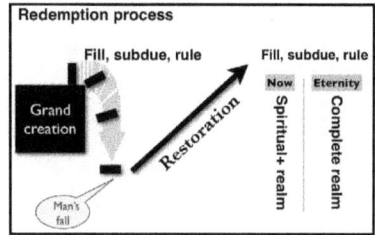

9) Reflect on the way God wants His people to 'work' for Him. What special insights do we gain from Isaiah 42:5-7? Why didn't Adam and Eve originally have this kind of assignment?

10) What does salt and light stand for in Matthew 5:13-16?

11) Look at the cross cultural missionary chart (p. 223) and make at least two observations.

   ✦

   ✦

12) The Book of Revelation several times states that we, God's people, are His kingdom and priests. What do those two roles mean? How do they work out in your life?

   ✦

   ✦

13) How has God employed us in His kingdom work?

14) What are one or two verses that remind you of God's desire to work in your life?

15) His people are now royal priests (salt/light). How might that change the way you do things in your work, whether at home, on sport's field or on your job? Is work good or bad? What do you think and why?

Advanced Questions

1) Use two words to describe your work (whether student, housewife, corporate, ministry, etc.).

   ✦

   ✦

2) How does the way the world understands work differ from the way God wants His people to think of it?

3) How does becoming Christ's disciple reshape how one looks at his or her work?

4) Pick a country and study the growth of Christianity in that country and its relationship to the number of full-time workers in that country. Write a small report.

5) Why does God work through our simple and sinful lives when He could do such a better and quicker job?

#12 Study: Determined to Share His Holiness

Redemption Through the Scriptures

God has made us His own and therefore busies Himself with training us for holiness (Hebrews 12:4-11). Redemption does not make us perfect, but it does perfectly enable us to walk in the Spirit, completing God's will for our lives. Only by sharing His holiness can God speak to us without accompanying judgment.

Study Questions

1) From the first chapters of Genesis, how do we know that the Lord wants us to live completely holy lives? Explain as needed.

2) What common delusion mentioned in chapter 12 of the book about salvation has done the church great harm?

3) What is our hope of glory?

4) Why does closeness with God require holiness? Please explain.

5) Where did the phrase 'my people' start and how is it continued throughout the Bible?

6) What is the constant tension between God and man that runs through the Old and New Testaments?

7) How were the king's role to help God's people?

8) What was special about Phinehas, the grandson of Aaron?

9) 1 Peter 1:15-19 reminds us of our obligation to share in God's holiness. Why is this so important?

10) How is devotion similar and different from being holy?

11) In many cases God has warned His people, but they disobey. How seriously do you think the church today follows God's Word? What makes you draw this conclusion?

12) How much do you interpret what you do in life as being associated with God's sanctifying (making holy) your life?

Advanced Questions

1) What might you say to a person that adamantly states one's life (character) has nothing to do with his or her job? How is this related to the believer who doesn't care about his or her lifestyle?

2) List various ways that God through the Old and New Testaments enables His people to be close to Him while on earth. (Recommended: draw a rough time chart and identify the means God used.)

3) Contrast God's discipline of God's people at the very end of 2 Chronicles (i.e. captivity) and what the church faced in Revelations 2-3. How are they different or similar?

4) Relate any church discipline that you have personally witnessed. What happened? Was it handled well? Any reflections on it?

5) Would you say God is unfair to encourage discipline in the church? Why or why not?

#13 Study: Desire for a Loving Relationship

Redemption Through the Scriptures

God wants us to love Him! Why? So that we might respond to Him and enjoy our life in Him. God wants His people now to be filled with peace and joy (1 Th 5:18). This study on developing a heart for God can be quite extensive.

Study Questions

1) What people are you close to? Why is that so?

2) Do you agree that good character traits are important to good relationships? Explain why.

3) What does John 15:16 say about our relationship with God?

4) Write down at least three aspects of relationships gleaned from the Genesis 2:15-18 passage.

  ✦

  ✦

  ✦

5) From your experience do you think unbelievers think much about a personal relationship with God? What is your personal experience? When did you first think about your relationship with God?

6) What are some basic functions of personal relationships?

7) How did the fall affect our relationship with God? How do we know?

8) How does Genesis 6:1-8 show us that man's relationship with others also became corrupted?

9) Who are a few people from the Old Testament times that God was pleased with? Are there any hints to why God favored them?

✦

✦

10) What changed in Isaac and Jacob's lives to cause them to seek God? How do you know they later followed God?

11) How is being second born related to the new teaching of rebirth?

12) How does circumcision serve as an example of regeneration (rebirth)? Provide verses that support your view.

13) How would you describe the relationship God wants with man? Do you experience that? Explain.

14) How are your personal relationships positively affected by your restored relationship with God? Why do you think this is possible?

15) Summarize what you learned by examining your relationship with God and others in the last few years. Are they typified by a rich fellowship? What areas do you need to work on further?

Advanced Questions

1) Could Jacob have first chosen God? Did God only foresee that Jacob would choose him or did God actually work in Jacob's life to cause Him to seek Him?

2) Study Jacob's life and note the things he experienced and how his heart began to seek God. Make a chart.

3) The word regeneration is used two times in the scriptures (Mt 19:28; Titus 3:5). How is the term theologically used? How does this usage compare to its biblical usage?

4) Do the people of God today enjoy a rich relationship with the Lord? Why so?

5) The restored relationship with God should influence man's relationship with others. Why is this so? Give some verses that support this.

6) Identify a personal relationship which you would like to see develop. Think up at least two steps to follow this through and a time when you will do it. Write them down and do it!

✦

✦

#14 Study: Deeper Fellowship with our Lord

While much time is spent teaching God's plan and work to gain redemption in the church, precious little time is given to God's purpose for redemption. God's greatest joy is for us to come into His presence where we can share in His blessings and joy and bear His fruit. It is from this learned security in His presence where God's people largely learn to love others.

Study Questions

1) Good communication is a mark of intimacy. Are you a good communicator in personal relationships? Rate yourself and explain.

2) What are four main purposes for God's great redemption plan?

+

+

+

+

3) What is intimacy? How is this relevant to you when thinking about God and yoursself?

4) How did the Law (i.e. the Old Covenant) help man get closer to God?

5) What concern arises when God draws near to people? Why?

6) When did the Lord sanctify the Israelites to Himself?

7) What do we mean by the 'Big Switch'? Why did the Lord do that?

8) What does the tabernacle or temple have to do with this topic of intimacy?

9) What are the implications of the NT passage, "You are a temple of God" (1 Corinthians 3:16)?

10) What are two of the three points of Isaiah 53:12?

   ✦

   ✦

11) How does the marriage institution help us understand the main ingredients of intimacy. Name at least three relevant aspects.

   ✦

   ✦

   ✦

12) How does the Apostle Paul affirm the fact that intimacy with God is best understood through marriage?

13) How does the vine image from John 15 help us understand the intimate relationship that God desires to have with His people?

14) In what ways do you cultivate a relationship with God our Father through Jesus?

15) What is needed to have intimacy? Do you share those intimate times with Him? Explain.

16) Why do you think that abounding joy (John 15:11) comes from abiding in the Lord?

17) Have you ever thought of prayer as an intimate time with God: getting to know God more and Him knowing you more? Discuss.

Advanced Questions

1) What do we mean by the constant tension between God's desire to be intimate with man and God's need to judge man?

2) Spiritual disciplines like quiet times (daily meeting God in His Word and prayer) reflect how we relate to God. How often do you privately meet with him each week? How do you find those times?

3) Find a picture that explains the different parts of the temple so that you can understand it and relate our relationship with God through the tabernacle.

4) Search both the terms tabernacle and temple in the New Testament. See how the words are used.

5) What is an example of a time when you have sensed that inner joy from your intimate times with the Lord? What was so special about that time? If not, what might be holding you back from such times?

6) All personal times shared with spouses, friends and brothers and sisters are built on the model of grace shown in the way God calls His people closer to Him. Through gracious communication we are able to grow in our relationships to a point where we can learn, get excited, share pain and find healing. Do you open up your heart with others? Why or why not?

#15 Study: Summary of Redemptive Truths

Redemption Through the Scriptures

Show how the redemptive message progresses throughout Biblical revelation and culminates at the cross.

This book is a chronological approach to Christ's person and work as revealed in the scriptures. Because God's plan was predetermined before the foundation of the world, and because the Lord wants us to look forward to and believe in God's love for His people, the redemptive plan has been coded into key historical events and included in the scriptures so that when Jesus did come, we would not miss God's gift but respond to Him and welcome Him into our lives (John 1:12).

Study Questions

1) How is a biblical theology different from a systematic theology?

2) Is it possible to know your belief is right while others are wrong? Does it really matter?

3) What did Jesus mean by Luke 24:44? (Put it in your own words.) Why did He describe it this way?

4) Describe the Hebrew way of organizing the Old Testament scriptures.

5) The scripture states, "by the predetermined plan and foreknowledge of God" (Acts 2:23) Christ was offered up. What does it mean that Christ's horrible death was part of the plan of God?

6) Provide at least three Old Testament redemptive themes and scriptures that prove that the cross was not sudden or a surprise.

-

-

-

7) Clarify why sin and guilt are crucial parts of redemptive theology?

- Sin

- Guilt

8) How does God's faithfulness assure us of God's judgment?

9) How does God's faithfulness assure us of God's salvation for those who believe in Christ?

10) Why is it so important to stress that salvation is through faith?

11) Pick out one religion or cult and show how their teachings are different from the true gospel, that is, the redemptive teaching of Christ and His work on the cross.

12) Why is it so important for believers to have a good trust and knowledge of the scriptures? List out important teachings from your memory and verses to back it up.

Advanced Questions

1) Two interpretations of Luke 24:44 are given regarding, "All things which are written about Me ... must be fulfilled." What are they? Which is correct? Why?

2) Draw two diagrams differentiating the way the Jewish and English Bibles organize their (Old Testament) scriptures.

3) Write out your testimony by wrapping at least three aspects of redemptive truths into it.

4) Many religious people, including professing Christians, have an inaccurate view of salvation. How might you use

these different aspects of redemption to help a person
that believes he or she is saved by good works to know it
is only by faith in Christ?

5) Share the gospel with someone or relate to a recent
witnessing opportunity. What redemptive truths did you
mention? Which did not you not share? Why or why
not? (This assignment is not trying to persuade believers
to believe that they need to share all the points of
redemptive theology at once but to help them be
conscious of their conversations.)

6) List and briefly describe the essential truths, as you see it,
embraced by biblical redemptive theology (the gospel
truths).

7) List three biblical truths that are not part of the gospel
and why they are not.

   ✦

   ✦

   ✦

8) The cults often go astray by misunderstanding God's full redemption plan. Identify one cult and do some reading of that cult. Show the various ways they do not offer salvation because they compromise or do not teach critical theological redemptive points.

#16 Study: Summary of Redemptive Restoration

Redemption Through the Scriptures

God's redemptive plan focuses on the cross and effectiveness of God's work through Christ's suffering. Unless God's people escaped God's wrath and were made perfect through Christ's righteousness, that glorious fellowship with God and each other could never come into existence. God with the creation is eagerly awaiting for the great revealing of the sons of God (Romans 8:19).

Study Questions

1) Look at the adjacent diagram, *The Meaning of Redemption*, and explain the three segments. Bonus! What do the five pictures represent?

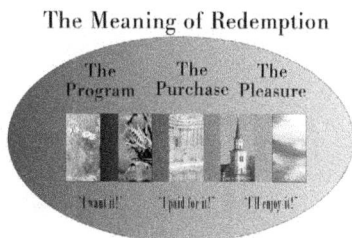
The Meaning of Redemption

The Program   The Purchase   The Pleasure

"I want it!"   "I paid for it!"   "I'll enjoy it!"

✦

✦

✦

2) What are two popular misconceptions that take the joy of salvation away from the people of God?

✦

✦

3) How would you summarize the purpose of this last chapter?

4) What are the two ongoing purposes for the grand redemption plan?

✦

✦

5) Faith is essential for our salvation, but how is the strength of our faith important to our Christian lives?

6) How do the two books of Genesis and Revelation work as one?

7) Explain the pattern of biblical revelation.

8) Briefly show how the 'new heavens and earth' is progressively revealed through the scriptures. Use the pattern above.

9) Relate at least two interesting aspects of the mountain and river theme.

-
-

10) What do the tabernacle and temple stand for? Why are they necessary?

11) Is there a temple in the first (Garden of Eden) or last Garden (New Jerusalem)? Explain.

12) Briefly show how the theme of light is progressively revealed through the scriptures.

13) What does Augustine state are the two purposes of marriage?

 ✦

 ✦

14) What is the third purpose, as suggested by the author? Why so?

15) How is marriage the apex of revelation? What is its spiritual meaning? Support yourself with biblical references.

16) Do you meet with God each day? Are they enjoyable times? Why or why not?

Advanced Questions

1) Summarize the meaning of redemption and how it relates to the purposes of redemption.

2) What knowledge would we lack and possible distortions arise without Genesis 1-3.

3) Read Genesis 1-3 and Revelation 20-22. How many common themes you can find?

4) Define and explain the pattern of biblical revelation. Take three themes and show how they are developed as one progresses through the biblical books. Do not take more than one page per topic.

5) Find a theme that is not listed and trace it through the scriptures.

6) Demonstrate how marriage highlights the two purposes of redemption. How does this expand your view of

marriage as well as your view of God's relationship with you?

7) Share one special thought you learned from this series on *Redemption Through the Scriptures.*

8) Share one practical way you were helped in your Christian life through this book.

9) Do you think you will still doubt God's care and love for you? If so, why?

Appendix: About the Author

Paul has worked as an overseas church planter during the 1980s and pastored in America during the 1990s. God called him to establish Biblical Foundations for Freedom in 2000 and since then he has been actively writing, holding international Christian leadership training seminars and serving in the local church.

Paul's wide range of books on Christian life, discipleship, godly living, leadership training, marriage, parenting, anxiety, Old and New Testament and other spiritual life topics provide special insights that are blended into his many books and media-rich training resources.

Paul has been married for more than thirty-five wonderful years. With eight children and three grandchildren, Paul and his wife Linda continually see God's blessings unfold in their lives.

For more on Paul and Linda and the BFF ministry, check online at:
www.foundationsforfreedom.net

www.ingramcontent.com/pod-product-compliance
Lightning Source LLC
Chambersburg PA
CBHW061753020426
42331CB00006B/1462